SPIRITUAL POVERTY

The Path to True Riches

*SIX STUDIES FOR GROUPS
OR INDIVIDUALS
WITH NOTES FOR LEADERS*

Jack Kuhatschek

INTER-VARSITY PRESS

INTER-VARSITY PRESS
38 De Montfort Street, Leicester LE1 7GP, England

British edition published by arrangement with Zondervan Publishing
House, Grand Rapids, MI 49530

First published 1993

British Library Cataloguing in Publication Data
A catalogue record for this book is available from the British Library.

ISBN 0-85111-366-4

Typeset and printed in the United States of America

*Inter-Varsity Press is the book-publishing division of the Universities and
Colleges Christian Fellowship (formerly the Inter-Varsity Fellowship), a
student movement linking Christian Unions in universities and colleges
throughout the United Kingdom and the Republic of Ireland, and a member
movement of the International Fellowship of Evangelical Students. For
information about local and national activities write to UCCF, 38 De
Montfort Street, Leicester LE1 7GP.*

Contents

The Beatitude Series

Welcome to the Beatitude Series. This series is designed to help you develop the eight character qualities found in those whom Jesus calls "blessed."

The Beatitudes are among the best-known and best-loved words of Jesus. They form the heart of the Sermon on the Mount, found in Matthew 5–7 and Luke 6:17–49. In eight brief statements Jesus describes the lifestyle that God desires and rewards:

> *Blessed are the poor in spirit,*
>   *for theirs is the kingdom of heaven.*
> *Blessed are those who mourn,*
>   *for they will be comforted.*
> *Blessed are the meek,*
>   *for they will inherit the earth.*
> *Blessed are those who hunger and thirst for righteousness,*
>   *for they will be filled.*
> *Blessed are the merciful,*
>   *for they will be shown mercy.*
> *Blessed are the pure in heart,*
>   *for they will see God.*
> *Blessed are the peacemakers,*
>   *for they will be called sons of God.*
> *Blessed are those who are persecuted because of righteousness,*
>   *for theirs is the kingdom of heaven.*

5

The Beatitudes turn the world's values upside down. We are tempted to say: "*Wretched* are the poor, for they have so little money. *Wretched* are those who mourn, for no one will hear their cries. *Wretched* are the meek, for they will be trampled by the powerful." Yet Jesus shatters our stereotypes and asserts that the poor will be rich, the mourners will be comforted, and the meek will inherit everything. What a strange kingdom he offers!

In recent years there has been some confusion about the kind of blessing Christ promises in these verses. The Beatitudes have been described as "God's prescription for happiness." One book has even called them "The Be-Happy Attitudes."

The Greek word *makarios* can mean "happy." J. B. Phillips translates the opening words of each beatitude, "How happy are . . . !" Nevertheless, John Stott writes:

> It is seriously misleading to render *makarios* "happy." For happiness is a subjective state, whereas Jesus is making an objective judgment about these people. He is declaring not what they may feel like ("happy"), but what God thinks of them and what on that account they are: they are "blessed."[1]

The eight guides in the Beatitude Series give you an in-depth look at each beatitude. But Jesus is not describing eight different types of people—some who are meek, others who are merciful, and still others who are peacemakers. He desires to see all eight character qualities in every one of his followers.

That's a tall order! Only those who enter Christ's kingdom by faith can expect such a transformation. And only those who serve the King can enjoy his rewards.

Our prayer is that The Beatitude Series will give you a clearer and deeper grasp of what it truly means to be blessed.

HOW TO USE THE BEATITUDE SERIES

The Beatitude Series is designed to be flexible. You can use the guides in any order that is best for you or your group. They are ideal for Sunday-school classes, small groups, one-on-one relationships, or as materials for your quiet times.

Because each guide contains only six studies, you can easily explore more than one beatitude. In a Sunday-school class, any two guides can be combined for a quarter (twelve weeks), or the entire series can be covered in a year.

Each study deliberately focuses on a limited number of passages, usually only one or two. That allows you to see each passage in its context, avoiding the temptation of prooftexting and the frustration of "Bible hopscotch" (jumping from verse to verse). If you would like to look up additional passages, a Bible concordance will give the most help.

The Beatitude Series helps you *discover* what the Bible says rather than simply *telling* you the answers. The questions encourage you to think and to explore options rather than merely to fill in the blanks with one-word answers.

Leader's notes are provided in the back of each guide. They show how to lead a group discussion, provide additional information on questions, and suggest ways to deal with problems that may come up in the discussion. With such helps, someone with little or no experience can lead an effective study.

SUGGESTIONS FOR INDIVIDUAL STUDY

1. Begin each study with prayer. Ask God to help you understand the passage and to apply it to your life.

2. A good modern translation, such as the *New International Version,* the *New American Standard Bible,* or the *New Revised Standard Version,* will give you the most help. Questions in this guide, however, are based on the *New International Version.*

3. Read and reread the passage(s). You must know what the passage says before you can understand what it means and how it applies to you.

4. Write your answers in the space provided in the study guide. This will help you to clearly express your understanding of the passage.

5. Keep a Bible dictionary handy. Use it to look up any unfamiliar words, names, or places.

SUGGESTIONS FOR GROUP STUDY

1. Come to the study prepared. Careful preparation will greatly enrich your time in group discussion.

2. Be willing to join in the discussion. The leader of the group will not be lecturing but will encourage people to discuss what they have learned in the passage. Plan to share what God has taught you in your individual study.

3. Stick to the passage being studied. Base your answers on the verses being discussed rather than on outside authorities such as commentaries or your favorite author or speaker.

4. Try to be sensitive to the other members of the group. Listen attentively when they speak, and be affirming whenever you can. This will encourage more hesitant members of the group to participate.

5. Be careful not to dominate the discussion. By all means participate! But allow others to have equal time.

6. If you are the discussion leader, you will find additional suggestions and helpful ideas in the leader's notes at the back of the guide.

Note

1. *The Message of the Sermon on the Mount* (Downers Grove, Ill.: InterVarsity Press, 1978), p. 33.

Introducing
Spiritual Poverty

Blessed are the poor in spirit,
for theirs is the kingdom of heaven.

In the movie *Fiddler on the Roof,* the main character, Tevye, tells the Lord: "I realize, of course, that it's no shame to be poor. But it's no great honor either!"

Most of us would agree wholeheartedly. Like Tevye, we ask: "So what would have been so terrible if I had a small fortune?" And we sympathize when he sings:

> If I were a rich man . . .
> I'd build a big, tall house with rooms by the dozen
> Right in the middle of the town,
> A fine tin roof and real wooden floors below.
> There would be one long staircase just going up,
> And one even longer coming down,
> And one more leading nowhere just for show.[1]

If you've seen the movie or heard the sound track, you are probably humming the melody in your mind right now. But before you burst into song, reflect on the sobering words of Jesus in the Sermon on the Mount: "Blessed are you who are *poor*" (Luke 6:20).

At first Jesus' statement seems completely illogical. How can shriveled children with distended bellies be considered "blessed"? What blessing is there in being homeless, hungry, and clothed in rags? The author of Ecclesiastes seems closer to the mark when he says: "A feast is made for laughter, and wine makes life merry, but money is the answer for every-thing" (10:19).

Yet Jesus often stands the world's logic on its head—not because he is illogical but because we are. Our thinking has become so distorted by sin that we often see things upside down, the opposite of the way God sees them.

How then are we to interpret this strange blessing? John Stott writes:

> The Old Testament supplies the necessary background against which to interpret this beatitude. At first to be "poor" meant to be in literal, material need. But, gradually, because the needy had no refuge but God, "poverty" came to have spiritual overtones and to be identified with hum-ble dependence on God. . . . The "poor man" in the Old Testament is the one who is both afflicted and unable to save himself, and who therefore looks to God for salva-tion.[2]

Jesus is speaking of a *spiritual* condition, not a material one. That is why Matthew writes, "Blessed are the poor *in spirit*" (5:3). Only those who admit their moral and spiritual bank-ruptcy receive God's blessing. Only those who come empty handed, admitting their need, will go away filled. According to Jesus, the kingdom of God will be populated not by the spiritually proud but by the spiritually poor—those who real-ize that they have no inherent right to be there. True spiritual poverty means humble dependence on God.

We must be cautious at this point, however, lest we com-pletely spiritualize Jesus' words. Those who are materially poor have usually been far more receptive to Christ than those who are rich. The common people, the prostitutes, the outcasts of society flocked to hear Jesus, while the rich and powerful plotted to kill him.

The poor often have no one to turn to but God. The rest of us are not so fortunate. We are tempted to trust in our money, our jobs, our education, and our accomplishments. Gradually, the gifts become more important to us than the Giver. We feel satisfied and secure—but for all the wrong reasons.

We need to hear Christ's stinging rebuke to the church at Laodicea: "You say, 'I am rich; I have acquired wealth and do not need a thing.' But you do not realize that you are wretched, pitiful, poor, blind and naked. I counsel you to buy from me gold refined in the fire, so that you can become rich; and white clothes to wear, so you can cover your shameful nakedness; and salve to put on your eyes, so you can see" (Rev. 3:17–18).

Spiritual poverty is an attitude we must cultivate daily. The six passages in this study guide help us develop a humble dependence on God. They strip away our pride and shatter our false sense of security.

But their purpose is not to wound but to heal. When we admit our poverty, God gives us true spiritual wealth. When we confess our nakedness, he gives us magnificent clothes to wear. And when we admit our blindness, God opens our eyes to see the rich blessings he offers those who are poor in spirit.

Jack Kuhatschek

Notes

1. Joseph Stein, "Fiddler on the Roof" (New York: POCKET BOOK, 1966), pp. 24–25.
2. John R. W. Stott, *The Message of the Sermon on the Mount* (Downers Grove, Ill.: InterVarsity Press, 1978), pp. 38–39.

1

Who Are the Poor?

MATTHEW 5:3; LUKE 6:20; 1:46–56

During a visit to Italy, a young and wealthy Theodore Roosevelt describes his encounter with a crowd of beggars:

> We hired one to keep off the rest. Then came some more fun. Papa bought two baskets of doughy cakes. . . . We tossed the cakes to them and we fed them like chickens with small pieces of cake and like chickens they ate it. . . . For a "Coup de Grace" we threw a lot of them in a place and [witnessed] a writhing heap of human beings. We made the crowds give us three cheers for the U.S.A. before we gave them cakes.[1]

After reading this account of the future president's "fun" in Italy, we cannot help but wonder who the poor were in that situation—the hungry children begging for cake, or the calloused benefactors tossing scraps to "chickens."

Nearly twenty percent of the 5.4 billion people on earth live in abject poverty. Yet the Bible teaches that a far deeper poverty afflicts us all, a poverty of spirit that we must acknowledge to receive God's blessing.

13

Purpose to grasp what it means to be poor In Spirit

1. Why do you think we often fear physical poverty more than spiritual poverty?

2. Read Matthew 5:3 and Luke 6:20. What differences do you note between these two beatitudes?

3. Some scholars claim that Matthew has spiritualized Jesus' original promise to the poor by adding the words "in spirit." How would you respond to that claim?

⮑ notes !

4. Read Luke 1:46–56. Mary contrasts two groups of people in her "song." Who are the ones she considers blessed?

herself – humble servant
those who fear him v 50
the humble v52   *Abraham + his*
the hungry v53   *descendant*
his servant Israel v54   *v55*

5. What types of people does Mary include in the other group?

Proud in their inmost thoughts v51
rulers from their thrones v82
The rich v 53

14

6. When you consider the descriptions of both groups, which fits you best? Explain.

7. Although the Messiah was still in Mary's womb, how would his coming bring a great reversal in the fortunes of these groups?

8. Why do you think Mary links poverty with humility (vv. 52–53) and wealth with pride (vv. 51–53)?

   Why is it natural for poverty to result in humility and wealth to result in pride?

9. If you are rich—at least by world standards—how can you guard yourself against pride and spiritual self-sufficiency?

Do we feel that we are sent away empty? sometimes? → could this be because we are spiritually poor but won't admit it? — Humility — how does this affect our relationship with god?

If you are poor, how can your poverty draw you closer to the Lord and his kingdom?

(do we think? because we aren't poor but think we are)
what is our attitude to real poverty
what about relationships with poor — bro Sis

10. How does Mary's song help you understand the meaning of Jesus' beatitude "Blessed are the poor in spirit"?

believers ha everything i common

11. Ask God to help you cultivate an awareness of your spiritual poverty. Pray your own song of praise to the Lord for the rich blessings you will receive.

BETWEEN STUDIES

In Matthew 6:19 Jesus tells us, "Do not store up for yourselves treasures on earth, where moth and rust destroy, and where thieves break in and steal. But store up for yourselves treasures in heaven, where moth and rust do not destroy, and where thieves do not break in and steal. For where your treasure is, there your heart will be also."

Think about what earthly treasures may have captured your heart. What can you do to loosen their grip on your life? What specific actions can you take this week to store up treasure in heaven?

Note

1. Edmund Morris, *The Rise of Theodore Roosevelt* (New York: Ballantine Books, 1979), p. 55.

2

Admitting Our Need

REVELATION 3:14–22

In C. S. Lewis's book *The Voyage of the Dawn Treader,* a nasty little boy named Eustace turns into an ugly, scaly, fire-breathing dragon. In desperation, he tries and tries to shed his dragon skin so that he can become a boy again. Finally, the great Lion, Aslan, approaches him and says:

> "You will have to let me undress you." I was afraid of his claws, I can tell you, but I was pretty desperate now. So I just lay flat down on my back to let him do it. The very first tear he made was so deep that I thought it had gone right into my heart. And when he began pulling the skin off, it hurt worse than anything I've ever felt. . . . Then he caught hold of me—I didn't like that much for I was very tender underneath now that I'd no skin on—and threw me into the water. It smarted like anything but only for a moment. After that it became perfectly delicious and as soon as I started swimming and splashing I found that all the pain had gone from my arm. And then I saw why. I'd turned into a boy again. . . . After a bit the lion took me out and dressed me—in new clothes—the same ones I've got on now.[1]

Both Scripture and experience confirm a fundamental principle—we must admit our need before Jesus Christ (or anyone else) can help us. In Revelation 3:14–22, the Lord helps us peel away our layers of hypocrisy.

1. Why do we often have such a difficult time admitting that we need help?

2. Read Revelation 3:14–22. Laodicea had no natural water supply. Nearby Colossae had cold, refreshing water, and Hierapolis had healing hot water. But by the time water was piped to Laodicea, it was lukewarm. How was the church of Laodicea like the city (v. 15)?

3. What does it mean to be spiritually lukewarm? (Give examples.)

Why do you think this condition is so nauseating to Jesus (v. 16)?

4. Laodicea was also the wealthiest city in Phrygia during Roman times. How had the city's wealth affected the church?

5. How might our personal or financial success deceive us and others about our true spiritual condition?

6. Laodicea took pride not only in its wealth but also in its famous eye salve and textile industry.[2] How does Jesus use these strengths of the city to rebuke the church (vv. 17–18)?

7. What might "gold refined in the fire," "white clothes," and "salve" symbolize in verse 18?

8. Jesus' rebuke and discipline are motivated by love (v. 19). In what specific ways can we repent from spiritual pride and apathy?

9. Although verse 20 is often used in gospel messages, how does Jesus' invitation apply to us as Christians?

10. Why does repentance always result in more intimate fellowship with Jesus?

11. What do you need to do to open the door to a deeper relationship with the Lord?

BETWEEN STUDIES

Take a moral and spiritual inventory this week. In what areas in your life might you be deceiving yourself and others about your true spiritual condition? Ask the Lord to peel away any layers of pretense and hypocrisy. Pray that you will have the strength to repent from spiritual pride or apathy.

Notes

1. C. S. Lewis, *The Voyage of the Dawn Treader* (New York: The Macmillan Company, 1952), p. 90.
2. Much of the background material for this study comes from *The NIV Study Bible* (Grand Rapids: Zondervan Publishing House, 1985), p. 1930.

3

Seeing Our Blindness

JOHN 9

The book *Flatland* describes a two-dimensional world that is the home of triangles, squares, rectangles, and circles. The author describes how difficult it is for the inhabitants of that land to understand or even believe in the three-dimensional world that lies beyond. When a sphere passes through their plane of existence, for example, it first appears as a point, then a circle that grows larger and larger, then smaller and smaller until it disappears.[1]

Throughout history, people of our world have had equal difficulty grasping the reality of the spiritual dimension. Some even deny that it exists. John 9 helps us open our eyes to things we often fail to see.

1. In the series Cosmos, astronomer Carl Sagen stated that the material universe is all that is or was or ever will be. What might lead some people to deny the existence of the spiritual world?

2. Read John 9. What does the disciples' question in verse 2 reveal about their beliefs?

How does Jesus clear up their confusion?

3. Instead of healing the man immediately, why do you think Jesus put mud on the man's eyes and told him to wash in the Pool of Siloam?

4. What is the connection between Jesus' spiritual claim, "I am the light of the world" (John 8:12), and his physical healing of a man blind from birth?

5. In what sense are we all spiritually blind from birth?

6. How do the Pharisees' conversations with the man expose their unwillingness to see the truth (vv. 13–34)?

7. What impresses you about the way this uneducated beggar stands up to the Pharisees?

8. Although the man was completely healed physically, how does his spiritual eyesight improve throughout this chapter (see vv. 11, 17, 33, 38).

9. What does Jesus mean when he says that he came so that "the blind will see and those who see will become blind" (v. 39)?

How does Jesus apply this statement to the Pharisees (vv. 40–41)?

10. According to this passage, what must we do to have our spiritual eyesight restored?

11. As Christians, what can we do to insure that our spiritual eyesight will grow sharper rather than dimmer with age?

12. Pray that the Lord will reveal your blind spots. Ask the Light of the world to clear up your distorted vision.

BETWEEN STUDIES

Make a list of several ways that spiritual blindness might reveal itself in non-Christians. Then make a separate list of the ways it might effect Christians.

Pray for a non-Christian you know, asking the Lord to touch that person's spiritual eyes. Ask a close friend or your spouse to pray for your spiritual eyesight throughout the week.

Note

1. Edwin A. Abbott, *Flatland* (New York: Harper & Row, 1983).

4

Seeking God's Mercy

LUKE 15:11–32

"Daddy, Chris pulled all the petals off the tulips!"

The announcement came from our daughter, Katie, who had decided to turn informant against her three-year-old brother, Chris.

I looked out our front window at our flower bed. Sure enough, there was a neat row of naked stems where once there had been tulips.

"Christopher James," I bellowed, "did you pull all the petals off the tulips?"

"No, dad," he replied innocently, "I didn't."

"Don't lie to me, son. I want you to tell me the truth. I won't spank you."

There was a long pause.

"Even if I *did* it?" he asked in amazement.

As Christians, we often imagine that our heavenly Father is perched with paddle in hand, ready to whack us every time

25

we step out of line. The parable of the lost son presents a very different picture. This story beautifully illustrates the reception we receive when we seek God's mercy.

1. Like Adam and Eve, why are we tempted to hide from God when we sin?

2. Read Luke 15:11–32. Based on the younger son's actions in verses 12–13, what might you conclude about his attitudes?

3. After his wealth was gone, why do you think the son stayed in the distant country rather than returning home immediately (vv. 14–16)?

4. In verses 17–20, the son "came to his senses." How does he illustrate what it means to be poor in spirit?

5. Imagine that the older son, rather than the father, had been the first one to see the younger son. How might the reception have been quite different?

6. In contrast, what is amazing about the reception the father gives his son (vv. 20–24)?

7. When you sin, do you expect God to act more like the father or the older brother? Explain.

8. What does the father in this parable teach us about our heavenly Father?

9. How does this portrait of the Father make you more inclined to seek his mercy when you sin?

10. What does the older son reveal about the dangers of self-righteousness?

11. How can we avoid having the older son's attitude toward Christians who blatantly sin and later seek forgiveness and restoration?

BETWEEN STUDIES

Think of Christians whom you have ridiculed or looked down on because of their spiritual failings (for example, TV evangelists). What does your superior and judgmental attitude reveal about your own spiritual condition? How does your attitude contrast with the father's attitude in the parable? Ask the Father to help you treat others with the same mercy that he has shown to you.

5

Treasure
in Heaven

MATTHEW 6:19–24

For seventeen years Mel Fisher searched for the legendary
Spanish galleon *Nuestra Señora de Atocha,* which sank mys-
teriously in 1622. Then one day his divers began waving their
arms and shouting: "We found it! We found it!"

"The silver . . . was stacked up like cordwood as far as the eye
could see." In the first two days, 40 divers brought up more
than 200 silver ingots, weighing 7 tons. Each bar was 15 in.
long and tipped the scales at about 70 lbs. Divers also found
the archetypal treasures of a shipwreck: wooden chests spill-
ing over with coins. . . . Estimates of the worth of the booty
range as high as $400 million. . . . "No one can say that this
isn't the greatest hit of all time."[1]

As children, most of us dreamed of discovering lost treasure.
Even as adults, we are fascinated with the thought of stacks of
silver, bars of gold, and chests full of coins and jewels. In Matthew 6:19–24, Jesus helps us see why treasure in heaven is
better than any treasure on earth.

29

1. Why do you think people as so fascinated with the idea of finding lost treasure, winning lotteries, and entering sweepstakes?

2. Read Matthew 6:19–24. What kinds of treasures do people tend to store up on earth?

3. According to Jesus, why is treasure in heaven a better investment than treasure on earth?

4. What examples can you give of today's treasure becoming tomorrow's junk?

5. How can materialism destroy our spiritual life (v. 21)?

6. In what practical ways can we store up treasure in heaven (see, for example, 1 Tim. 6:17–18)?

7. In a literal sense, how can good and bad eyes affect the quality of our lives (vv. 22–23)?

8. In Scripture, the eye is often used as a metaphor for the heart (see, for example, Ps. 119:10, 18). How might the focus of our lives affect the quality of our hearts?

9. If a slave tried to serve two masters, why would he end up being devoted to one and despising the other (v. 24)?

10. Whether we admit it or not, why will we end up despising God if we divide our loyalties between him and money (v. 24)?

11. How does storing up treasures on earth and serving money differ from wisely using and enjoying the gifts and resources God has given us (see Prov. 6:6–11; Luke 12:15; 1 Tim. 4:4; 6:17)?

12. To what extent do you feel that money and possessions are hindering your loyalty to God?

How can you stop serving money and restore God to his rightful place in your life?

BETWEEN STUDIES

Reflect on the ways in which money and possessions have become masters to be served rather than resources to be used and enjoyed. To what extent are you trying to satisfy spiritual longings in material ways? Ask God for help in breaking materialism's grip on your life. Reaffirm your commitment and loyalty to him.

Store up treasure in heaven this month by giving some of your resources to those in need.

Note

1. "We Found It! We Found It!" *Time,* August 5, 1985, pp. 21–22.

6

When the Poor Become Kings

ISAIAH 65:17–25

In a chapter entitled "Why Job Died Happy," Philip Yancey writes:

> For people who are trapped in pain, or in a broken home, or in economic misery, or in fear—for all those people, for all of us, heaven promises a time far longer and more substantial than the time we spent on earth, of health and wholeness and pleasure and peace. . . .
>
> The Bible never belittles human disappointment, . . . but it does add one key word: temporary. What we feel now, we will not always feel. Our disappointment is itself a sign, an aching, a hunger for something better. And faith is, in the end, a kind of homesickness—for a home we have never visited but have never stopped longing for.[1]

In Isaiah 65:17–25 we get a glimpse of that time and place where all our longings will be satisfied and all our dreams will be fulfilled.

1. What longings or hopes or dreams do you expect to be fulfilled in the kingdom of God?

2. Read Isaiah 65:17–25. What clues indicate that Isaiah's promises apply both to Israel's return from captivity and to the future Messianic kingdom?

3. In the new heavens and new earth what "former things" (v. 17) will never again trouble God's people?

4. Isaiah knew about the end of death (see 25:8). Why then do you think he speaks only of long life in this chapter rather than eternal life?

5. In what other ways will the heavens and earth be "new"?

6. What appeals to you about Isaiah's vision of life in God's kingdom?

7. What similarities do you see between this passage and the parallel passage in Revelation 21:1–8?

8. What differences do you note between these two passages?

9. How do these visions of the new heavens and new earth compare to popular concepts of heaven or life after death?

10. In what ways do these visions of God's kingdom make you "homesick"?

11. Throughout this study guide, you have meditated on the meaning of the first beatitude: "Blessed are the poor in spirit, for theirs is the kingdom of heaven." How would you summarize what it means to be poor in spirit?

12. Based on your study of Scripture, why are the poor in spirit truly blessed by God?

13. Thank God for the rich blessings that are yours in Jesus Christ. Ask him to mold and shape you into the kind of person described in the beatitudes.

BETWEEN STUDIES

Without realizing it, people often seek to fill spiritual longings in material ways. They try to satisfy the ache in their heart with food, entertainment, or the latest purchase on their "wish list."

Try to identify specific areas in your life in which you are trying to fill spiritual longings in material ways. What evidence do you see in your life that these material solutions are not working? What deeper, spiritual needs are you really seeking to fill?

Bring each of these needs to God. Ask him to show you which of these needs he can satisfy now and which ones will only be fully satisfied when Jesus returns.

Note

1. *Disappointment with God* (Grand Rapids: Zondervan Publishing House, 1988), pp. 246–47.

Leader's Notes

Leading a Bible discussion—especially for the first time—can make you feel both nervous and excited. If you are nervous, realize that you are in good company. Many biblical leaders, such as Moses, Joshua, and the apostle Paul, felt nervous and inadequate to lead others (see, for example, 1 Corinthians 2:3). Yet God's grace was sufficient for them, just as it will be for you.

Some excitement is also natural. Your leadership is a gift to the others in the group. Keep in mind, however, that other group members also share responsibility for the group. Your role is simply to stimulate discussion by asking questions and encouraging people to respond. The suggestions listed below can help you to be an effective leader.

PREPARING TO LEAD

1. Ask God to help you understand and apply the passage to your own life. Unless that happens, you will not be prepared to lead others.

2. Carefully work through each question in the study guide. Meditate and reflect on the passage as you formulate your answers.

37

3. Familiarize yourself with the leader's notes for the study. These will help you understand the purpose of the study and will provide valuable information about the questions in the study.

4. Pray for the various members of the group. Ask God to use these studies to make you better disciples of Jesus Christ.

5. Before the first meeting, make sure each person has a study guide. Encourage them to prepare beforehand for each study.

LEADING THE STUDY

1. Begin the study on time. If people realize that the study begins on schedule, they will work harder to arrive on time.

2. At the beginning of your first time together, explain that these studies are designed to be discussions, not lectures. Encourage everyone to participate, but realize that some may be hesitant to speak during the first few sessions.

3. Read the introductory paragraph at the beginning of the discussion. This will orient the group to the passage being studied.

4. Read the passage aloud. You may choose to do this yourself, or you might ask for volunteers.

5. The questions in the guide are designed to be used just as they are written. If you wish, you may simply read each one aloud to the group. Or you may prefer to express them in your own words. Unnecessary rewording of the questions, however, is not recommended.

6. Don't be afraid of silence. People in the group may need time to think before responding.

7. Avoid answering your own questions. If necessary, rephrase a question until it is clearly understood. Even an

eager group will quickly become passive and silent if they think the leader will do most of the talking.

8. Encourage more than one answer to each question. Ask, "What do the rest of you think?" or "Anyone else?" until several people have had a chance to respond.

9. Try to be affirming whenever possible. Let people know you appreciate their insights into the passage.

10. Never reject an answer. If it is clearly wrong, ask, "Which verse led you to that conclusion?" Or let the group handle the problem by asking them what they think about the question.

11. Avoid going off on tangents. If people wander off course, gently bring them back to the passage being considered.

12. Conclude your time together with conversational prayer. Ask God to help you apply those things that you learned in the study.

13. End on time. This will be easier if you control the pace of the discussion by not spending too much time on some questions or too little on others.

Many more suggestions and helps are found in the book *Leading Bible Discussions* (InterVarsity Press). Reading it would be well worth your time.

STUDY 1
Who Are the Poor?
MATTHEW 5:3; LUKE 6:20; 1:46–56

Purpose: To begin to grasp what it means to be "poor in spirit."

Question 1 Every study begins with an "approach question," which is discussed *before* reading the passage. An approach question is designed to do three things.

First, it helps to break the ice. Because an approach question doesn't require any knowledge of the passage or any special preparation, it can get people talking and can help them to warm up to each other.

Second, an approach question can motivate people to study the passage at hand. At the beginning of the study, people in the group aren't necessarily ready to jump into the world of the Bible. Their minds may be on other things (their kids, a problem at work, an upcoming meeting) that have nothing to do with the study. An approach question can capture their interest and draw them into the discussion by raising important issues related to the study. The question becomes a bridge between their personal lives and the answers found in Scripture.

Third, a good approach question can reveal where people's thoughts or feelings need to be transformed by Scripture. That is why it is important to ask the approach question *before* reading the passage. The passage might inhibit the spontaneous, honest answers people might have given, because they feel compelled to give biblical answers. The approach question allows them to compare their personal thoughts and feelings with what they later discover in Scripture.

Question 3 "Since Luke speaks simply of 'the poor,' many have concluded that he preserves the true teaching of the historical Jesus—concern for the economically destitute—while Matthew has 'spiritualized' it by adding 'in spirit.' The issue is not so simple. Already in the OT, 'the poor' has religious overtones . . . those who because of sustained economic privation and social distress have confidence only in God (e.g., Pss. 37:14; 40:17; 69:28–29, 32–33; Prov 16:19 . . .). Thus it joins with passages affirming God's favor on the lowly and contrite in spirit (e.g., Isa 57:15; 66:2). This does not mean there is lack of concern for the materially poor but that poverty itself is not the chief thing. . . . Yet, though poverty is neither a blessing nor a guarantee of spiritual rewards, it can be turned to advantage if it fosters humility before God" (D. A. Carson, *The Expositor's Bible Commentary: Matthew* [Grand Rapids: Zondervan Publishing House, 1984], p. 131).

Questions 4–5 In addition to herself (whom she describes as God's humble servant), Mary mentions "those who fear him" (Luke 1:50), "the humble" (v. 52), "the hungry" (v. 53), "his servant Israel" (v. 54), and "Abraham and his descendants" (v. 55).

In the other group she mentions "those who are proud in their inmost thoughts" (v. 51), "rulers from their thrones" (v. 52), and "the rich" (v. 53).

Question 7 The great reversal brought by the Messiah will scatter the proud (v. 51), bring down rulers (v. 52), and send the rich away empty (v. 53). But the humble will be lifted up (v. 52), the hungry will be filled (v. 53), and Israel will be helped (vv. 54–55).

Question 8 See note to question 3.

STUDY 2
Admitting Our Need
REVELATION 3:14–22

Purpose: To realize that being "poor in spirit" means admitting our needs to God.

Question 2 Christ's statement that "I wish you were one or the other" is often misinterpreted. People assume that he wanted the Laodiceans to either be spiritually cold (that is, against him) or spiritually hot or "on fire" (that is, for him). Yet both cold and hot are good in this context. Christ wants his people to either be like the cold, refreshing waters of Colossae or like the healing hot waters of Hierapolis. Instead, the Laodiceans had no good properties to commend themselves.

Question 4 Like the city, the church in Laodicea assumed that it was rich and wealthy and did not need a thing (v. 17). Their wealth had brought both pride and a dangerous sense of self-sufficiency.

Question 6 Its "strategic position made Laodicea an extremely prosperous commercial center, especially under Roman rule. . . . It was an important center of banking and exchange. It distinctive products included garments of glossy black wool, and it was a medical center noted for ophthalmology. . . . The church was self-sufficient rather than half-hearted. Like the city, it thought it had 'need of nothing'. In fact, it was spiritually poor, naked and blind, and needed 'gold', 'white garments' and 'eyesalve' more effective than its bankers, clothiers and doctors could supply" (*New Bible Dictionary,* Second Edition [Wheaton, Ill.: Tyndale House, 1982], p. 681).

Question 9 Although it is normally assumed that Christ is speaking to unbelievers who need to open their hearts to Christ, the context suggests that he is speaking to the self-deluded believers in the church of Laodicea. "Like citizens inhospitable to a traveller who offers them priceless goods, the Laodiceans had closed their doors and left their real Provider outside. Christ turns in loving appeal to the individual" (*New Bible Dictionary,* p. 681).

STUDY 3
Seeing Our Blindness
JOHN 9

Purpose: To realize that those who are poor in spirit must see their own blindness.

Question 2 "The rabbis had developed the principle that 'There is no death without sin, and there is no suffering without iniquity.' They were even capable of thinking that a child could sin in the womb or that its soul might have sinned in a preexistent state. They also held that terrible punishments came on certain people because of the sin of their parents. As the next verse shows, Jesus plainly contradicted these beliefs" (*The NIV Study Bible,* p. 1614).

Question 3 Jesus may have put mud on the man's eyes and asked him to wash in the Pool of Siloam in order to stimulate the man's faith and get him to express his faith in action. See 2 Kings 5:1–14 for a similar situation.

Question 4 Jesus often linked a spiritual claim to a physical miracle. For example, he claimed to be the bread of life and fed the five thousand (John 6), he claimed to be the light of the world and healed the blind man (John 9), and he claimed to be the resurrection and the life and raised Lazarus from the dead (John 11). The miracles not only substantiated his claims but also were physical illustrations of spiritual truths.

Question 8 The man "progressed in his thinking about Jesus: from a man (v. 11), to a prophet (v. 17) who might be followed by disciples (v. 27), to one 'from God' (v. 33), to one who was properly to be worshiped (v. 38)" (*The NIV Study Bible,* pp. 1614–15).

Question 9 Those who come to Jesus in humility, admitting their spiritual blindness, will be given sight. But those who proudly claim to be able to see without Jesus' help (such as the Pharisees), will be exposed for what they really are— spiritually blind.

STUDY 4
Seeking God's Mercy
LUKE 15:11–32

Purpose: To see how the study of the lost son beautifully illustrates the reception we receive when we seek God's mercy.

Question 2 "The 'share of the estate' (v. 12) that a younger son would receive on the death of the father would be one-third,

43

because the older (or oldest) son received two-thirds, a 'double portion'—i.e., twice as much as all other sons (Deut. 21:17). If the property were given, as in this case, while the father lived, the heirs would have use of it (cf. v. 31); but if they sold it, they could not normally transfer it as long as the father lived. . . . The son may have been asking (v. 12) for immediate total ownership, but the parable does not specify the exact terms of the settlement. The property was 'divided'; so the elder son was made aware of his share (cf. v. 31)" (Walter L. Liefeld, *The Expositor's Bible Commentary: Luke* [Grand Rapids: Zondervan Publishing House, 1984], p. 983).

The fact that the son made the highly unusual request for his inheritance before the father had died indicates an insensitivity and lack of propriety. The fact that he took all his possessions, leaving nothing behind, may indicate that he wanted to be totally independent of his father's authority. Finally, the fact that he went to a distant country and squandered his wealth indicates irresponsibility and a lack of moral character.

Question 4 The son realizes his need ("I am starving to death," v. 17), his sin ("Father, I have sinned against heaven and against you," v. 18), his unworthiness ("I am no longer worthy to be called your son," v. 19), and his need to return to the only one who could help him ("I will set out and go back to my father," v. 18). In each area the son illustrates the true meaning of "poor in spirit."

Question 6 "The son's speech was never completed (v. 21). Instead the father more than reversed the unspoken part about becoming a 'hired man' (v. 19). The robe, ring and sandals (v. 22) signified more than sonship . . . the robe was a ceremonial one such as a guest of honor would be given, the ring signified authority, and the sandals were those only a free man would wear [slaves went barefoot]" (Liefeld, *Luke*, p. 984).

Questions 7–8 When we sin, we often expect God to reject us and to require us to do some sort of penance before we can be restored. The father in this parable beautifully portrays the true response we can expect: the Father welcomes and embraces us. He doesn't even wait for our little speech about our sin. Instead, he throws a party to celebrate our return! In the previous parable of the lost coin, Jesus comments, "In the same way, I tell you, there is rejoicing in the presence of the angels of God over one sinner who repents" (vv. 8–10).

STUDY 5
Treasure in Heaven
MATTHEW 6:19–24

Purpose: To understand why treasure in heaven is better than any treasure on earth.

Question 2 In Greek, the present tense "Do not store up for yourselves treasure on earth" could be translated "Stop storing up for yourselves treasure on earth." Jesus calls his disciples to have a decisive break with the world's lifestyle, which constantly devotes itself to the acquisition of things.

Question 3 John Stott writes: "The earthly treasure we covet, Jesus reminds us, 'grows rusty and moth-eaten, and thieves break in to steal it' (NEB). The Greek word for 'rust' (*brosis*) actually means 'eating'; it could refer to the corrosion caused by rust, but equally to any devouring pest or vermin. Thus in those days moths would get into people's clothes, rats and mice eat the stored grain, worms take whatever they put underground, and thieves break into their home and steal what they kept there. Nothing was safe in the ancient world. And as for us moderns, who try to protect our treasure by insecticides, rat poison, mouse-traps, rustproof paints and burglar alarms, it disintegrates instead through inflation or devaluation or an economic slump. Even if some of it lasts through this life, we can take none of it with us to the next. Job was right: 'naked I came from my mother's womb, and naked shall I return.' But 'treasure in heaven' is incorruptible" (*Sermon on the Mount,* pp. 155–56).

Question 4 Encourage people to think of actual examples of things that they wanted desperately, but that later held little value for them.

Question 5 Jesus warns us that if we fill our lives with earthly treasures, we will find it increasingly difficult, if not impossible, to focus our hopes and energies on him and his kingdom. Materialism and godliness cannot coexist.

Questions 7–8 The word "good" (v. 22) can mean either "single" in the sense of undivided loyalty or generous and liberal. Likewise "bad" (v. 23) can mean evil or miserly and selfish. D. A. Carson writes: "Jesus is therefore saying either (1) that the man who 'divides his interest and tries to focus on both God and possessions . . . has no clear vision, and will live without clear orientation or direction' (Filson)—an interpretation nicely compatible with v. 24; or (2) that the man who is stingy and selfish cannot really see where he is going; he is morally and spiritually blind—an interpretation compatible with vv. 19–21" (*Matthew,* p. 178).

Question 9 We normally assume that "things" are our tools or toys, purchased to serve our needs. In contrast, Jesus implies that those who devote themselves to serving money will become enslaved by it. They will cross the line where their possessions no longer serve them but instead become their master. Ironically, we can become possessed by our possessions!

Question 11 "It is important to face squarely and honestly the question: what was Jesus prohibiting when he told us not to lay up treasure for ourselves on earth? It may help if we begin by listing what he was (and is) not forbidding. First, there is no ban on possessions in themselves; Scripture nowhere forbids private property. Secondly, 'saving for a rainy day' is not forbidden to Christians, or for that matter a life insurance policy which is only a kind of saving by self-imposed compulsion. . . . Thirdly, we are not to despise, but rather to enjoy, the good things which our Creator has given us richly to enjoy. . . . What Jesus forbids his followers is the *selfish accumulation of goods* (NB, 'Do not lay up for yourselves treasures on earth'); extravagant and luxurious living; the hardheartedness which does not feel the colossal need of the world's underprivileged people; the foolish fantasy that a person's life consists in the abundance of his possessions; and the materialism which tethers our hearts to the earth" (Stott, *Sermon on the Mount,* pp. 154–55).

STUDY 6
When the Poor Become Kings
ISAIAH 65:17–25

Purpose: To get a glimpse of the new heaven and new earth— the place where all our longings will be satisfied and all our dreams fulfilled.

Question 2 The prophecies in this chapter seem deliberately ambiguous. On the one hand, they offer hope to the exiles in Babylon. The Lord promises them that "the former things [that is, their painful captivity] will not be remembered" (v. 17). Likewise Jerusalem, which lay in ruins during the captivity, will be restored ("I will create Jerusalem to be a delight," v. 18). Even the people's servitude in captivity seems to be in view in verses 22–23 ("No longer will they build houses and others live in them, or plant and others eat. . . . They will not toil in vain or bear children doomed to misfortune"). Yet Isaiah's prophecies go far beyond Israel's earthly restoration from Babylon. The Lord will create a "new heavens and a new earth" (v. 17). People will have the longevity of Adam and his early descendants (v. 20). And the wolf and the lamb will feed together, while the lion will eat straw like an ox (v. 25). These are pictures of life in the messianic kingdom.

Question 4 This passage is perplexing. As mentioned previously, Isaiah's language may be deliberately ambiguous so that his promises would apply both to Israel's restoration from captivity and to their ultimate deliverance during the messianic kingdom.

Question 7 These two passages are similar in many ways. Both mention the new heavens and new earth (Isa. 65:17; Rev. 21:1). In both passages the authors use similar language to declare that "the former things will not be remembered" (Isa. 65:17) or "the old order of things has passed away" (Rev. 21:4). Likewise, Jerusalem figures prominently in both passages (Isa. 65:18–19; Rev. 21:2).

Question 8 The differences between these passages is also striking. Isaiah refers simply to "Jerusalem" (Isa. 65:18–19), whereas John speaks of "the new Jerusalem," which comes down out of heaven from God (Rev. 21:2). John also refers to the new Jerusalem "as a bride beautifully dressed for her husband" (Rev. 21:2). There is a much greater emphasis in Revelation on God dwelling forever with his people (vv. 3–4), who will be his children (v. 7). And where Isaiah uses the imagery of long life, John clearly states that "there will be no more death" (Rev. 21:4). There are several other contrasts between these passages that you and your group can explore.

Question 9 Popular notions of life after death usually refer simply to "heaven." Heaven is properly portrayed as the dwelling place of God and his angels and is often thought of as our eternal home. Yet although the Scriptures teach that we go to be with the Lord in heaven after we die (see 2 Cor. 5:6–8; Phil. 1:21–23), heaven is not our final home, nor do we live eternally as disembodied spirits. We will dwell in resurrected bodies (1 Cor. 15:12–58; 1 Thess. 4:13–18) on a renewed earth, as Isaiah and John have stated. At that time heaven will come down to earth, and God will dwell with us eternally.